Collins English Library   Level 4

HUCKLEBERRY FINN

MARK TWAIN

Abridged and simplified by Lewis Jones

Illustrations by Isabelle Montgomery

Collins: London and Glasgow

This edition © Lewis Jones 1978

Published in Great Britain by
William Collins Sons and Co Ltd
Glasgow G4 0NB

Printed by Martins of Berwick

First published in the Collins English Library, 1978
Reprinted: 1982, 1983, 1984, 1985, 1986, 1987, 1988

ISBN 0 00 370069 0

We are grateful to American History Picture Library
for permission to reproduce the photograph
which appears on the cover.

Collins English Library

Series editors: K R Cripwell and Lewis Jones

A library of graded readers for students of English as a second or foreign language, and for reluctant native readers. The books are graded in six levels of difficulty. Structure, vocabulary, idiom and sentence length are all controlled according to principles laid down in detail in A Guide to Collins English Library. A list of the books follows. Numbers after each title indicate the level at which the book is written: 1 has a basic vocabulary of 300 words and appropriate structures, 2 : 600 words, 3 : 1000 words, 4 : 1500 words, 5 : 2000 words and 6 : 2500 words.

Huckleberry Finn

This story tells of life in America about 1840. At that time negroes in the Southern States of America were still slaves. Negro slaves were bought by white people who then made them work. The negroes did not get any money for this work, but they did get a bed and food. Huckleberry Finn and Jim lived in one of these Southern states — Missouri. So Jim was Mrs Watson's slave. Across the Mississippi river from Missouri were the Northern states of Illinois, Indiana and Ohio. Here negroes were free men. Jim wanted to escape to one of these Northern states in order to have his freedom.

There were serious punishments in the South for helping a slave to escape to freedom in a Northern state. So Huckleberry Finn was placing himself in some danger.

1

You don't know about me, unless you've read a book by the name of "The Adventures of Tom Sawyer". But that doesn't matter.

That book was made by Mr Mark Twain, and he told the truth (mainly). The way that the book ends up is this — Tom and me, we found the money that the thieves hid in the cave, and it made us rich. We got six thousand dollars each — all gold.

Well, Judge Thatcher, he took it and kept it for us. We got a dollar a day each out of it, all the year round.

Old Mrs Douglas took me for her son, and said she would teach me good manners and proper behaviour. She put me in new clothes, and I felt all tied-up tight. She rang a bell for supper, and you had to come on time. When you got to the table, you couldn't just start eating. She used to lower her head and whisper things over the food, and you had to wait for her.

And she wouldn't let me smoke: she said it wasn't clean. That's just the way with some people. They start forbidding things when they don't know anything about them.

Her sister, Miss Watson, had just come to live with her. She was a thin old maid with big glasses. Miss Watson used to say, "Don't put your feet up there, Huckleberry," and "Don't sit lazy like that, Huckleberry — sit up straight," and "Why don't you try to behave?" Then she told me about the place where bad people go, and I said I wished I was there. She got angry then.

My dad hadn't been seen for more than a year, and that was all right by me. I didn't want to see him any more. He always used to beat me when he hadn't been drinking. So I used to stay out in the woods when he was around.

Well, three or four months ran along, and it was well into the winter. I'd been to school almost all the time, and I could read and write, just a little. I could multiply up to six-times-seven-is-thirty-five. And when I got tired of school, I just stayed away.

Miss Watson thought black people should give thanks to God, and ask for forgiveness every day. So at night the negroes were brought in. And them and Miss Watson, they all thanked God for everything, and then everybody went off to bed.

Miss Watson's negro, Jim, had a hair-ball as big as your hand. It had come out of the fourth stomach of a cow, and he used to do magic with it. The hair-ball talked to Jim, and Jim told it to me.

He says, "Your old father — he doesn't know yet what he's going to do. Sometimes he thinks he'll go away, and sometimes he thinks he'll stay. But the best way for you is to rest easy, and give yourself no trouble worrying about him."

When I lit my candle and went up to my room that night, there sat dad, his own self!

I had shut the door, and there he was. I used to be frightened of him all the time, he hit me so much. But now, after the first shock, I wasn't frightened of him, hardly at all.

He was about fifty, and he looked it. His hair was long and messy and oily, and you could see his eyes shining through. It was all black, no grey, and so was his beard.

There was no colour in his face: it was white. Not like another man's white, but a white to make you sick: dead-fish white. His clothes were old and torn, and two of his toes had pushed out of his boot. I stood a-looking at him: he stood there a-looking at me.

Then he says, "Smart-looking clothes — very. You think you're pretty much of a big cheese, *don't* you?"

"Maybe I am, maybe I ain't," I says.

"Don't you give me none of your big mouth," says he. "You're educated, too, they say — can read and write. You think you're better than your father now, don't you, 'cause he can't? Just looky here — you drop that school, you hear? Your mother couldn't read and write either. None of the family could. And you ain't going to give people the idea you're better than your father — you hear? Ain't you a sweet-smelling flower though? A bed and bed-clothes — and your own father's got to sleep outside in

9

the leather-maker's yard. I never saw such a son. They say you're rich. Hey? How's that?"

"They lie — that's how."

"Looky here — don't you give me any of that smart tongue. You give me that money tonight. I want it."

"I ain't got any money."

"It's a lie. Judge Thatcher's got it. You get it. Say — how much have you got in your pocket? I want it."

"I've only got a dollar, and I want that to...."

"You just give it out."

He took it, then he went down town to get some whisky. He drank so much, he didn't know what he was doing. He said he'd hit me till I was black and blue, if I didn't get some more money for him. I borrowed three dollars from Judge Thatcher, and dad took it and got drunk again.

Every time he took money, he got drunk. And every time he got drunk, he raised up trouble around town. And every time he raised up trouble, he got put in prison.

One day in the spring, he said to me, "I'll show you who's boss, me or Huck Finn."

He caught me and took me up the river about five kilometres, in a little boat. We crossed over to the Illinois shore, where there weren't any houses — only a little wood cabin.

The forest there was real thick, so you couldn't find the cabin if you didn't know where it was. He kept me with him all the time, and I never got the chance to run off. We lived in that old cabin for days, and he always locked the door and put the key under his head, nights.

He had a gun (which he'd stolen, I suppose), and we fished and hunted, and that was how we lived. Every little while, he locked me in, and went down to the store, five kilometres away.

When he'd caught fish, and shot some animals or birds, he sold them for whisky. He fetched it home and got drunk and had a good time, and beat me.

It was kind of lazy and comfortable all day, smoking and fishing, and no books or study. Two months or more ran along, and my clothes got to be all tears and dirt. And I didn't have to wash or comb, or eat on a plate like with old Mrs Douglas. It was pretty good times up in the woods there.

But dad was getting too free with his stick, and there were marks all over me. He started going away so much too, and locking me in. Once he was gone three days. It was terrible lonely.

I decided I would fix up some way to leave there. I hunted through the place over a hundred times, and at last I found something — an old wood-saw without any handle, up in the roof. I oiled it and went to work.

An old horse-blanket was nailed against the wall at the far end of the cabin, behind the table. I raised the blanket, and started to saw through the wooden wall. I was nearly finished when I heard my dad's gun in the woods. I

11

dropped the blanket and hid my saw.

After supper that night, dad took up the whisky, and drank and drank. In the middle of the night there was a terrible scream. Dad looked wild, and he was jumping around the cabin and shouting.

"Snakes!" he screamed. "Take them off. They're biting me on the neck."

But I couldn't see any snakes. He chased me round and round the place with a knife. He said I wanted to kill him, so he would have to kill me first.

But pretty soon he was tired out, and dropped against the door and fell asleep.

2

"Get up!"

It was after sun-up, and I'd been asleep. Dad was standing over me.

"Out with you," he said, "and see if there's a fish on the lines for breakfast."

He unlocked the door and I went up the river bank. Some tree-branches were coming down-river, so I knew the water was beginning to rise.

Then all at once here comes an empty boat — a canoe about four metres long. A beauty. I jumped head-first off the bank, clothes and all, and I swam out to the canoe. I climbed in and brought her in to the shore.

Dad wasn't in sight yet, and then I had an idea. I ran the canoe into a place where the tree-branches hung down and hid her, and I said nothing about it to dad.

The river was coming up pretty fast, and that afternoon some lengths of wood came sailing along. Dad insisted on selling them in the town across the river. So he locked me in and went off in the boat.

I got out my saw and went to work again. Before he was on the other side of the river, I was out of the hole. I took the bag of corn-meal and put it in the canoe. Then I did the same with the bacon, then the whisky. I took all the coffee and sugar, and the gun, and my old saw and two buckets and the coffeepot and fish-lines and matches — I took everything that was any use.

I fixed the piece of wall back in its place. Then I had an idea. I went into the woods with dad's gun, and shot a wild pig. I smashed in the cabin door, then I cut the throat of the pig and laid him on the floor to bleed.

I filled an old bag with big rocks, and pulled it from the cabin door through the woods, then I sank it in the river. You could easily see the marks on the ground from the cabin to the river bank.

I pulled out some of my hairs and dropped them in the blood, then I threw the pig in the river. I cut a hole in the bottom of the bag of corn-meal, and I carried it about a hundred metres across the grass, through the trees east of

14

the cabin, to a shallow lake.

The corn-meal made a line on the ground all the way to the lake. I tied up the hole in the meal bag and took it to the canoe again. It was about dark now, so I smoked a pipe and waited for the moon to rise.

I says to myself: they'll follow the marks of the bag of rocks to the shore, and search the river bottom for my body. And they'll follow the corn-meal to the lake, and look for the thieves that killed me. But they won't hunt up and down the river. So I can sail anywhere I want to.

Jackson's Island is good enough for me.

When the moon was bright, I was lying in the bottom of the canoe, travelling down the middle of the river. It didn't take me long to get to Jackson's Island, about four kilometres downstream.

The island stood up in the middle of the river, big and dark and solid, like a great boat without any lights. I ran the canoe into the bank towards the Illinois shore. I had to push the hanging branches to one side to get in, and nobody could have seen the canoe from the river.

There was a little grey in the sky now. So I stepped into the woods, and laid down for a sleep before breakfast.

3

The sun was up high when I wakened. I got my traps out of the canoe and made a nice camp in the thick woods. I made a kind of tent out of my blankets. Then I caught a cat-fish and opened him with my saw. Towards sundown I started my camp fire and had supper.

And so on for three days and nights.

But the next day, I went exploring the island. I was boss of it. It belonged to me, and I wanted to know all about it.

Daylight was just coming up when I caught a sight of fire, away through the trees. I went towards it, careful and slow. A man laid there with a blanket round his head. Pretty soon he rolled over and put out his arms, and threw off the blanket.

It was Miss Watson's Jim!

I sure was glad to see him. I says, "Hello Jim!"

He jumped up and stared at me. Then he drops down on his knees and says, "Don't hurt me — don't! I always liked dead people. You go and get in the river again, where you belong. Don't do anything to old Jim, that was always your friend."

Well! I soon made him understand I wasn't dead!

And Jim says, "But looky here, Huck, who was it that was killed in the cabin, if it wasn't you?"

So I told him the whole thing.

Then I says, "How do you come to be here, Jim?"

He didn't say anything for a minute, then he says, "Maybe I'd better not tell."

"Why, Jim?"

"Well, I — I *run off.*"

"Jim!"

"Well, you see, it was this way. One night pretty late, I was listening outside the door. And I hear Miss Watson say she's going to sell me down in Orleans. She didn't want to, but she could get eight hundred dollars for me. And that's a big pile o' money. Old Mrs Douglas tried to tell her she didn't ought, but I never waited to hear the rest. I got out pretty quick, I tell you.

"When it come dark, I walked into the river, and push a piece o' wood in front o' me. Then a raft of big boards comes sailing down, all tied together. And I climbed on. When the raft came past the island here, I got off and landed. I had my pipe and some matches in my cap, and they weren't wet, so I was all right."

The island was only four kilometres long and a quarter of kilometre wide. About the middle there was a hill about twelve metres high. We climbed all over it, and we found a good big cave in the rock. It was almost up at the top, on the side towards Illinois.

The cave was as big as two or three rooms all together, and Jim could stand up straight in it. We took some fish off the lines and began to get ready for dinner. We spread the blankets inside for a carpet, and ate our dinner in there. We put all the other things at the back of the cave.

The river went on rising and rising for ten or twelve days, till at last it was over the banks. One night we caught a part of a raft — nice wooden boards. It was four metres wide and about five metres long — a solid level floor.

One night, just before daylight, here comes a wooden house down the river, on the west side. She was leaning over, considerable. We went out in the canoe and climbed into the house at an upstairs window. In the first daylight we could see a bed, and a table, and two old chairs. And something like a man was laying on the floor, in the far corner.

So Jim says, "Hello, you!"

But he didn't move. So I shouted again, and then Jim says, "That man ain't asleep — he's dead."

He went and bent down and looked, and says, "It's a dead man. Yes indeedy. And no clothes on. He's been shot in the back. Don't look at his face, Huck — it's too horrible."

I didn't look at him at all. There were plenty of old cards lying about the floor, and old whisky bottles. There were two old dresses, and a woman's sun-hat and clothes, and some men's clothes too.

We put the lot into the canoe. And we got an old tin lamp, and a shiny new knife, and a lot of candles, and a tin cup, and buttons, and some nails, and some bottles of medicine, and a fish-line, and a horse-shoe. And just as we were leaving, Jim found a wooden leg. And so it was a pretty good find.

All the way back we had no accidents and didn't see anybody. We got home all safe.

4

Well, the days went along, and the river went down between its banks again. Things were getting slow and not very interesting.

So one morning I judged I would go over the river, and find out what was happening. Jim said, couldn't I put on some of those old things, and dress like a girl?

That was a good idea. So we shortened one of the dresses, and I turned up my trouser legs to my knees. I put on the sun-hat and tied it under my chin.

I started up the Illinois shore in the canoe just after dark. At the other side I tied up the canoe and started along the bank. There was a light burning in a little cabin, and I looked in at the window. There was a woman about forty years old in there. She was making wool into a ball by the light of a candle on a wooden table.

I didn't know her face, so I knocked at the door.

"Come in," says the woman, and I did.

She says, "Take a chair." I did it. "What might your name be?"

"Sarah Williams."

"Where abouts do you live?"

"In Hookville, twelve kilometres below. I've walked all the way. My mother's sick, and I've come to tell my uncle Abner Moore. I ain't ever been here before. Do you know him?"

"No. I haven't lived here quite two weeks. You'd better stay here all night."

"No," I says. "I'll rest a while, and then go on."

She talked about her husband, and her relations up the river — and so on and so on. But pretty soon she got to my dad and the murder.

"Some think old Finn did it himself," she says. "Most everybody thought that at first, but before night they changed around, and judged it was done by a runaway black boy named Jim."

"But *he*...." I stopped. I thought I'd better keep quiet, and she ran on.

"The negro ran off the same night Huck Finn was killed. There's three hundred dollars for anybody that finds him. And two hundred dollars for anybody that finds old Finn too. Some people think the negro ain't far from here. Hardly anybody goes over to Jackson Island over there. I was pretty certain I'd seen smoke over there. My husband's going over to see — him and another man."

I had got uneasy and my hands were shaking. "Is your husband going over there tonight?"

"Oh yes. They'll go over after midnight. The negro'll likely be asleep, and they can hunt up his camp fire."

The woman kept looking at me pretty strangely, and I didn't feel a bit comfortable.

Pretty soon, she says, "What did you say your name was, honey?"

"M — Mary Williams."

"Honey, I thought you said it was Sarah?"

"Oh yes, ma'am, I did. Sarah Mary Williams."

Well, the woman started talking about the rats that ran about the place. She said she had to throw things at them, and she showed me a bit of metal. She told me to try and hit one of the rats.

When the first rat showed his nose I threw good and hard. If he'd stayed still, he'd have been a sick rat. She said that was real fine, and I would probably get the next one. I sat down. She dropped the metal on to my knees, and I banged my legs together on it.

Then she looked me straight in the face, but very pleasant, and says, "Come now — what's your real name? Is it Bill, or Tom, or Bob?"

I was shaking like a leaf, and I didn't know what to do.

"Now I ain't going to hurt you. You must tell me your secret — I'll keep it. Tell me all about it now — that's a good boy."

So I says I'll tell her everything. "I had to work for a nasty old farmer in the country, fifty kilometres from the river. And he was so cruel to me, I had to run away. I stole some of his daughter's clothes, and left. I've travelled at night and hid in the daytime. I was trying to find my uncle Abner Moore."

She says, "Say — when a cow's laying down, which end of her gets up first? Answer quick now."

"The back end, ma'am."

"Well then, a horse?"

"The front end, ma'am."

"Which side of a tree does the most green grow on?"

"North side."

"Well, it seems you *have* lived in the country. What's your real name now?"

"George Peters, mum."

"Well, try to remember it, George. And don't go among women in that old dress. When you throw at a rat or anything, stand up tall and bring your hand up over your head. And miss your rat by one or two metres. Throw with a straight arm from the shoulder — like a girl. Not with your arm out to one side, like a boy.

"And when a girl tries to catch something between her knees, she throws the knees apart. She doesn't bang them together, like you with that piece of metal. Now run along to your uncle, Sarah Mary Williams George Peters."

I went up the bank to where my canoe was. I jumped in and was off in a hurry. When I got to the cave, Jim was asleep on the ground.

I says, "Get up and move yourself, Jim! There

22

ain't a minute to lose. They're after us!"

Jim never asked any questions, he never said a word. In half an hour everything we had in the world was on our raft. I tied the canoe to it, then we pushed quietly out into the river.

Soon the island was behind us.

5

The raft seemed to go very slow. We needed a tent. So Jim took up some of the top boards, and built a comfortable wigwam to keep us dry. Right in the middle of the wigwam we laid down about fifteen centimetres of dirt. This was to build a fire on, in cold or rainy weather.

We fixed up a short stick to hang the lamp on — we always had to light the lamp when a big steamboat was coming downstream.

Every night I used to go on shore at some little village, and buy corn-meal or bacon or other stuff to eat. Sometimes I lifted a chicken that was sitting comfortable, and took him along.

Moving before daylight, I went into the fields and borrowed some new corn. And now and then we shot a water-bird that got up too early in the morning (or that didn't get to bed early enough in the evening). We caught fish, and took a swim now and then, and sometimes we just talked.

I was telling Jim that French people talked different to us: "You couldn't understand a word they said, Jim — not one word."

"How's that?"

"*I* don't know: but it's so. Suppose a man came up to you and said, '*Polly-voo franzy*' — what would you think?"

"I wouldn't think anything. I'd bang him over the head — if he wasn't white. I wouldn't allow any negro to call me that."

"He ain't calling you anything. He's only saying 'Do you know how to talk French?' "

"Well why couldn't he *say* it?"

"He *is* saying it."

"Well, it's foolish talk. There ain't no sense in it."

"Looky here Jim. Does a cat talk like we do?"

"No. A cat doesn't."

"Well, does a cow?"

"No, they don't."

"They talk different from each other, and different from us. It's only natural and right, ain't it?"

"Of course."

"Well then, ain't it natural and right when a *Frenchman* talks different from us? You answer me that."

"Is a cat a man, Huck?"

"No."

"Is a cow a man? Or is a cow a cat?"

"No."

"Well, then. Naturally she doesn't talk like

25

each of them. Is a Frenchman a man?"

"Yes."

"*Well* then, why doesn't he talk like a man? You answer me *that*!"

It was no use wasting words — you can't teach a negro to argue. So I gave up.

We judged that three nights more would fetch us to Cairo, and the bottom of Illinois, where the Ohio River comes in. We would sell the raft and get on a steamboat there, and go away up the Ohio among the free States, and then be out of trouble.

I began to get it into my head that Jim was almost *free* — and who was to blame for it? *Me.* I says to myself, "What has poor Miss Watson ever done to you? The poor woman tried to teach you your books, and tried to teach you good manners, she tried to be good to you. *That's* what she did. And now you're seeing her negro go off in front of your eyes, and you never say one word against it."

Jim said, "As soon as I get to a free State, I'll save all my money and not spend a cent. And when I've got enough, I'll buy my wife — she works on a farm close to Miss Watson's. Then we'll both work to buy the two children. And if their master won't sell them, I'll get somebody to go and steal them."

I could hardly believe I was hearing such talk. He'd never dared to talk such talk in his life before. Here was this negro going to steal his children — children that belonged to a man I didn't even know, a man that hadn't ever hurt me.

Jim sings out, "Pretty soon I'll be shouting for happiness. And I'll say, it's all because o' Huck. I'm a free man, and Huck did it. Jim won't ever forget you, Huck. You're the best friend Jim ever had. And you're the *only* friend Jim's got now."

Well, I felt bad and low. Then I thought to myself: suppose you give Jim up, would you feel better? No, says I. I would not. Well then, says I, you can just stop worrying about it.

We passed a town before daylight, but it was high ground. No high ground about Cairo, Jim said.

I says, "Maybe we already went by Cairo in the dark one night."

When it was daylight, here was the clear Ohio water near the shore, sure enough. So that was the end of Cairo. We couldn't take the raft upstream of course. We could only wait for dark, and start back in the canoe.

So we slept all day among the trees. And when we went back to the raft about dark, the canoe was gone!

6

It was a huge big river down there — sometimes almost two kilometres wide. We sailed downriver at nights, and stopped and hid the raft during the day. Then we set out the fish-lines, and had a swim in the river, to get fresh and cool.

At night we pushed the raft out to the middle, and let the river take her where it wanted. Then we lit our pipes, and hung our legs in the water, and talked about all kinds of things.

After midnight the people on shore went to bed, and then for two or three hours the shore was black — no more points of light in the cabin windows. The points of light were our clock — the first one that showed meant that morning was coming, so we hunted for a place to hide and tie up.

One morning, about daybreak, I found a canoe, and I crossed over to the main shore. I paddled about a kilometre up a stream among the woods, to find something to eat.

Just as I was passing a kind of cow-path, a couple of men came running up the path as fast as they could go. I thought they were coming after me — or maybe Jim. But they sang out and begged me to save their lives.

They said they were being chased — and there were men and dogs a-coming. They jumped into the canoe, and in a few minutes we heard the dogs, and the men shouting. As we got further and further away, we could hardly hear them at all. And by the time we reached the river, everything was quiet. We hid in the cotton-woods and we were safe.

One of those fellows was about seventy or

more, and had a bald head and a few grey hairs. He had an old hat on, and a dirty blue woollen shirt, and a pair of torn old blue trousers. Over his arm he had a long old blue coat with shiny metal buttons. And both of them had big fat travelling-bags.

The other fellow was about thirty, and he was dressed just about as ordinary.

After breakfast we all talked. And the first thing that came out was — these chaps didn't know each other.

"What got you into trouble?" says the baldhead to the other chap.

"Well, I'd been selling something to clean the hard stuff off the teeth. And it does take it off — and generally it takes the outside of the teeth with it. But I stayed about one night longer than I ought to. I was just trying to get out quietly when I ran into you, this side of town. That's the whole story — what's yours?"

"Well, I'd been holding meetings there — speaking against drink — and I was a great favourite of the women, big and little. I was taking as much as five or six dollars a night — ten cents each, children and negroes free — and business was growing all the time. Then a little report got around last night — it said I enjoyed a private glass of whisky when I'm by myself. A negro woke me up this morning and said the people were getting together with dogs and horses. I didn't wait for any breakfast — I wasn't hungry."

"Old man," says the young one, "I think we

might make a team. What do you think?"

"I've got nothing against it. What work do you do — mainly?"

"I'm a printer. Sell a few medicines. Theatre-actor. Teach singing and geography for a change. Oh, I do lots of things. Almost anything, if it ain't work.

"I've done considerable doctoring in my time. And I tell people's past and future pretty good — when somebody finds out the facts for me. Church meetings too — I put them on at different places. But I have come down in the world, gentlemen. I, who was so high."

"Down from where?" says the baldhead.

"Gentlemen," says the young man, with serious eyes, "you would not believe me. The secret of my birth...."

"The secret of your birth?"

"Gentlemen, I will tell it to you. In truth I am a duke."

Jim's eyes almost shot out of his head when he said that, and I suppose mine did too.

Then the baldhead says, "No!"

"Yes. My great-grandfather was the oldest son of the Duke of Bridgwater. He came to this country about the end of the last century, to breathe the pure air of freedom. When he died, his second son wrongly took the title and the lands. The first son — the real duke — was my grandfather. I am the rightful Duke of Bridgwater. And here I am, with no lands, hunted by men, pushed to one side by the cold world, heart-broken. And now forced to share the company of low fellows on a raft."

And he began to cry. Jim pitied him, and so did I. We tried to comfort him, but it was no use. But he said we could call him by his proper title if we liked. And we ought to bend low when we spoke to him. And someone should bring his dinner and do things for him. Well, that was easy, so we all did it. But the old man didn't look very comfortable about it all.

"Bathwater," he says, "I'm sorry for you, but you ain't the only person that's had troubles like that."

"No?"

"No. You ain't the only person that's made a secret of his birth."

And now *he* began to cry. "Bathwater, will you keep my secret if I tell you?" he says.

"Till death!" He took the old man by the arm.

"Bathwater, I am the King of France."

Jim and me, we just stared this time.

Then the Duke says, "You are what?"

"Yes, my friend, it is true. At this moment your eyes are looking at Louis the Seventeenth."

"You! At your age! No! You must be six or seven hundred years old at least."

"Trouble has done it, Bathwater. Trouble has brought these grey hairs, and this baldness. Yes gentlemen, you see before you the lonely, suffering, rightful King of France."

Well, he cried again, so Jim and me, we tried to comfort *him*. But he said it was no use, but we could go down on one knee when we spoke to him. And give him his meals before anyone else. And not sit down till he asked us. So Jim and me, we did all these things for him, and he got happier.

I soon made up my mind that these two weren't kings or dukes at all, but just liars. But I never said anything. It's the best way. If they wanted us to call them kings and dukes, I didn't mind.

That was one thing I learned from my dad. With his kind of people, it's best to let them have their own way.

7

They asked us a considerable lot of questions. "Why do you cover up the raft this way?" "Why do you hide in the daytime?" And — "Is Jim a runaway negro?"

Says I, "Would a runaway negro run *south*?" But I had to explain Jim somehow, so I says, "Me and my dad, we were coming downriver with our negro Jim. We were all going to live with my Uncle Ben, about seventy kilometres below Orleans. One night, a steamboat ran over the corner of our raft. We all went into the water, but my dad was drunk — he never came up again.

"For the next day or two, people came up and tried to take Jim away from me. They believed he was a runaway negro. We don't sail in the daytimes any more. At nights they don't worry us."

The duke says, "Leave me alone to think out a plan. Then we can travel in the daytime if we want to."

There was a little town about five kilometres below the bend, and after dinner the duke said he would go into town and fix something.

He found a little printing office in the town. It was empty at the time and no doors were locked. So he spent the day there. He printed a few little jobs for farmers in that printing office — bills for horses. And he got in a few dollars worth of advertisements for the newspaper.

He took in nine dollars and a half, and he said he'd done a pretty good day's work for it. Then he showed us another little job he'd printed. It had a picture of a runaway negro with a stick over his shoulder. The reading was all about Jim, and just described him exactly. Anybody who caught him (it said) would get two hundred dollars.

"Now," says the duke, "after tomorrow we can sail in the daytime. When anybody comes, we can tie Jim up with a rope, and lay him in the wigwam. We can say we caught him up the river, and we're going to get the money."

We all thought the duke was pretty clever. We pushed out about ten o'clock that night, and we sailed pretty wide away from the town.

About four in the morning, Jim says, "Huck, d'you think we're going to come across any more kings on this trip?"

"No," I says.

"Well," says he, "that's all right then. This one's drunk, and the duke ain't much better."

One morning, we came in sight of another little town in a big bend, so we tied up about a kilometre away.

The duke got some big sheets of paper and some black paint, and he wrote on them:

At the village hall —

FOR THREE NIGHTS ONLY!

The world-famous actors

DAVID GARRICK!

and

EDMUND KEAN!

of the London theatres

in their exciting play

THE ROYAL NONESUCH!!!

Then he stuck the sheets up all over the village. At the bottom of the sheet was the biggest line of all — which said: LADIES AND CHILDREN NOT ALLOWED.

"There," says he, "that line'll fetch them!"

Well, all day the king was hard at work, putting up a stage and a curtain and a line of candles. And that night the hall was full of men in no time. When the place couldn't hold any more, the duke stood up before the curtain.

He told them it was the *grandest* play that ever was. And Edmund Kean was the most *wonderful* actor. When they were all excited enough, he rolled up the curtain.

The king came running out on his hands and knees, with no clothes on at all. And he was painted all over in rings and lines of every colour. It was terrible funny, and the people almost killed themselves laughing.

And when the king had finished, he danced off the stage, and they shouted and banged their feet and laughed *haw-haw* till he came back again. They made him do it again, and then another time. Well, it would have made a cow laugh.

Then the duke lets the curtain down and raises his arms. He says this great play will be given only two nights more. It is on its way to London, where the seats are sold already.

Then he says, "I hope you've all enjoyed the show. And I hope you'll mention it to your friends."

Twenty people sings out, "What? Is it over? Is that *all*?"

The duke says yes. Then there was a fine time. Everybody shouts out. "It's all lies! We've been tricked!" And they rose up and started a-going for that stage.

But a big fine-looking man jumps up on a seat and shouts, "Hold on! Just a word, gentlemen." They stopped to listen. "All right, we've been fooled. But we don't want to be laughed at by this whole town, do we? *No*. We want to go out of here quiet, and tell people it was a great show. Then *we* can laugh at the *rest* of the town. Doesn't that make sense?"

"It sure does! — The judge is right!" everybody shouts out.

"All right then — not a word about any trick. Go along home, and tell everybody to come and see the show."

Next day you could only hear one thing around the town — what a wonderful show it was. The hall was full again that night, and we fooled the crowd the same way. The third night it was full again, but they weren't newcomers this time — they were people that were at the show the other two nights.

I stood by the duke at the door, and I saw that every man had full pockets, or something under his coat. I smelt bad eggs and sickly cabbages and such things. And if I know a dead cat, there were sixty-four of them too.

Well, when the place was full, the duke gave a fellow twenty-five cents and told him to watch the door. Then he took me round a corner, and said, "Walk fast now till you get away from the houses. And then run for the raft like the devil himself!"

I did it and he did the same. We hit the raft at the same time, and edged towards the middle of the river. The king comes out from under the wigwam and says, "Well, how did the old thing work out this time, duke?"

The duke says, "Fools! Flatheads! I *knew* they'd be ready for us, the third night. They can all have a picnic now if they want to — they brought plenty supplies!"

We never showed a light till we were about

fifteen kilometres below the village. Then we had supper, and the king and the duke laughed their bones loose. Those fellows took in 465 dollars in those three nights. I'd never seen so much money all in one place before.

When they were both asleep, Jim says, "Doesn't it surprise you, the way these kings behave, Huck?"

"No," I says, "it doesn't."

"Why doesn't it, Huck?"

"Well, it doesn't, because it's in the blood. I guess they're all alike."

"But Huck, these kings of ours, they're real bad jokes."

"Well, that's what I'm a-saying. All kings are real bad jokes, as far as I can see."

I went to sleep.

8

Next day, we stopped where there was a village on each side of the river. The duke and the king began to set up a plan for working on those two towns. They wanted to try the Nonesuch again, because there was so much money in it. But they judged it wouldn't be safe — the news might have reached along the river by this time.

So at last the duke said he'd set his brains to work, and take a look at the Arkansaw village. And the king, he said he'd try the other village, without any plan, but just wait for some good ideas to come along.

We'd all bought new store clothes where we stopped last. And now the king put his on, and he told me to put mine on. The king's clothes were all black, and he looked real smart and straight-backed: a grand and good old man.

There was a big steamboat laying at the shore about five kilometres above town. Says the king, "Since I'm dressed real fine, maybe I'd better arrive on the steamboat, like from St Louis or Cincinnati or some other big place."

Then we saw a simple-looking young country fellow, sitting by the shore on a dead tree. He had a couple of big cloth bags by him, and he was resting in the powerful warm sunshine.

"Run the canoe in shore," says the king. I did it. "Where are you on your way to, young man?"

"For the steamboat. Going to Orleans."

"Come into the canoe," says the king. "The boy here will help you with those heavy bags. Jump out and help the gentleman, Adolphus." (Meaning me.)

I did it, and the three of us started on again. The king said he was on his way to see an old friend on a farm. And the young fellow says, "When I first saw you, I said to myself, *It's Mr Harvey Wilks, sure, but he's just a bit too late*. You ain't him, are you?"

"No. But I'm sorry if Mr Harvey Wilks has missed anything."

"Well, he's missed seeing his brother Peter die.

38

Peter's talked about nothing else, these past three weeks. He hasn't seen his brother Harvey since they were boys together. And he hasn't seen his brother William at all — William can't hear and he can't speak."

"Did anybody send to Harvey and William?"

"Oh yes, a month or two ago, when Peter was first sick — he knew he wasn't going to get well. He left a letter behind for Harvey, and it said where he's hid his money."

"Why hasn't Harvey come, then? Where does he live?"

"Oh, he lives in England. Sheffield. Man o' the church. He hasn't ever been in this country. He mightn't have got the letter at all, you know."

"Too bad, too bad. You're going to Orleans, you say?"

"Yes, but that's only a part of it. I'm going in a ship next week for Rio de Janeiro. My uncle lives there."

"It's a pretty long journey. I wish I was going. Got any children, has he, this Peter Wilks?"

"He leaves three of them — all girls. Mary Jane's nineteen — she's the red-headed one. Susan's fifteen. And Joanna's about fourteen — that's the plain one that does all the good works."

"Poor things! Left alone in the cold world!"

"Well, they could be worse. Old Peter had friends. Hobson and Lot Hovey and Ben Rucker and Abner Shackleford and Levi Bell the lawyer and Dr Robinson...."

39

Well, the old man went on asking questions till he emptied that young fellow. He asked about everything and everybody in the whole town. Then he says, "Was Peter Wilks well-off?"

"Oh yes, pretty well-off. He had houses and land, and probably three or four thousand in cash hidden somewhere."

"When did you say he died?"

"I didn't say, but it was last night."

"And they're burying him today, likely?"

"Yes. About the middle of the day."

When we got to the steamboat, the young chap left us. And the king says to me, "Now you go off and fetch the duke here. And tell him to make it fast. Go on. Push off."

When I got back with the duke, the king told him the whole story. Then he says, "The brother William can't hear and he can't talk. Can you act that, Bathwater?"

The duke said he'd acted that on the stage before. So then they waited for a steamboat. Late that afternoon a big one came along, and the king called out and we all got in. When we got to the village, they sent us to the shore in a little boat.

About twenty men came crowding along when they saw us, and the king says, "Can any of you gentlemen tell me where Mr Peter Wilks lives?" They looked at each other and nodded their heads. Then one of them says, soft and gentle, "I'm sorry, sir. But we can only tell you where he *did* live yesterday evening."

Suddenly the king broke down and fell

against the man, and put his head on his shoulder and cried all down his back.

And he says, "Oh no! Dear me, no! Our poor brother — gone. And we never got to see him. Oh, it's too *too* hard!"

Then he turns round, and makes a lot of foolish signs on his hands to the duke. And then *he* dropped a bag and started to cry. Well, the men gathered round, and said all sorts of kind things. They carried the bags up the hill for them, and let them lean on them and cry.

These two were the trickiest pair I ever saw. It made me ashamed of the human race.

9

The news was all over the town in two minutes, and you could see the people running from every which way. Pretty soon we were in the middle of a crowd, and the noise of all the feet was like a soldier-march. The windows and doorways were full. And every minute somebody would shout, "Is it *them*?"

When we got to the house, the street in front of it was packed with people, and the three girls were standing in the door. Mary Jane *was* red-headed, but that made no difference — she was real beautiful. Her face and eyes were all lit up like sunrise, she was so glad her uncles had come.

The king, he spread his arms, and Mary Jane, she jumped for them, and plain Joanna jumped for the duke. And everybody (at least the women) cried for happiness.

Then the king looked round for the wooden box with the body in it. The coffin was over in a corner, on two chairs. So then him and the duke, they put a hand across each other's shoulder, and the other hand across their eyes. And they walked sad and slow over there.

And all the talk and noise stopped; and people said "Shhh!" The men took their hats off and lowered their heads.

And when the two of them got there, they bent over the coffin and looked in at Peter. Then they burst out a-crying so you could hear them in Orleans almost. Then they put their arms round each other's necks, and hung over each other's shoulders. And then for three or four minutes I never saw men lose so much water.

And everybody was doing the same. And the place was so wet, I never saw anything like it.

Then the king got down on his knees at one side of the coffin, and the duke at the other side, and they rested their heads against the wooden box, and the king whispered out loud some real godly thoughts. And so everybody broke down and started crying again.

I never saw anything so shameful.

Well, the king, he gets up and pours out a lot of foolishness — all about the long journey of seven thousand kilometres and sweetness and kind friends and his poor departed brother. And all that kind of rubbish. It was just sickening.

Then somebody in the crowd started up a church tune, and everybody sang it with him. Music *is* a good thing, and after all that word-butter and pig-soup, it was nice and fresh and honest.

Then the king invited all the friends of the family to supper with him that evening, and he named Mr Hobson and Lot Hovey and Mr Ben Rucker and Abner Shackleford and Levi Bell and Dr Robinson....

And people shook hands with the duke, who didn't say anything. He just made signs with his hands and said, "Goo-goo goo-goo," like a baby that couldn't talk.

Then Mary Jane fetched the letter her father had left. And the king read it out loud and cried over it. It gave the house and three thousand dollars in gold to the girls. And it gave the leather-yard business, with some other houses and land (worth about seven thousand), and three thousand dollars in gold, to Harvey and William. And it told where the six thousand cash was hidden, down in the room under the house.

So these two snakes said they'd go and fetch it up, and they told me to come with a candle. We went down and shut the door behind us, and then they found the bag, and poured the money out on the floor. It was a lovely sight, all those little yellow chaps.

The king's eyes did shine! He laughs and says, "Oh, Bathwater, this beats the Nonesuch, eh?"

Almost everybody would have just accepted a pile of money like that. But not these two. Oh no, they had to *count* it. And it comes out 415 dollars short.

"We want to take this money upstairs and count it in front of everybody. Then there's nothing suspicious. But when the dead man says there's six thousand dollars, and we can only show...."

"Hold on," says the duke. "We've got money. Let's make it up to six thousand."

He starts to pull the yellow chaps out of his pocket, and the king does the same. They had almost nothing left, but they made up the six thousand clear.

"Say," says the duke, "I've got another idea. Let's go upstairs and count this money, and *give it to the girls*."

"That is the most wonderful idea that ever a man had! Let them fetch along their suspicions now!"

When we got upstairs, the king counted the money in front of everybody. Then he gives out another flood of fine words, and says, "Friends all, my poor brother there always did well by his family in this valley of sorrows. And now these poor little lambs are left fatherless and motherless. Do you think we would steal — yes, *steal* — from those poor sweet lambs at such a time? Here, Mary Jane, Susan, Joanna, take the money — take it *all*. It's the gift of him that lies cold over there."

Then there was such jumping and tears and

kissing as I never did see. But then a big iron-faced man came forward and laughed right in the king's face. Everybody was shocked.

"Doctor!" they says.

And Abner Shackleford says, "Robinson, ain't you heard the news? This is Harvey Wilks."

The doctor turned to the king and says, "An Englishman? *You*? It's the worst copy of an Englishman I ever heard. *You* — Peter Wilks's brother? Don't make me laugh."

Well! How they all crowded round the doctor and tried to quiet him, and explain to him.

Mary Jane straightened herself up, and she says, "*Here* is my answer to that." She puts the bag of money into the king's hands, and says, "Take this six thousand dollars, and put it into any business you like, for me and my sisters. And don't give us any receipt for it."

But Dr Robinson says, "All right. I'll have nothing to do with it. But I'm warning you. Soon you're going to feel sick when you think of this day."

And away he went.

"All right, doctor," says the king. "When they're sick, we'll send for you."

10

That night they had a big supper. And after, me and plain Joanna had supper off the left-overs in the kitchen. And she began asking me some uncomfortable questions about England.

She says. "Did you ever see the king?"

"Well of course. He goes to our church."

"I thought he lived in London?"

"Well, he does."

"But I thought *you* lived in Sheffield?"

I thought quick while I coughed on a chicken bone. "I mean, he goes to our church when he's in Sheffield. That's in summertime, when he comes to take the sea-baths."

"Well, how you talk — Sheffield ain't on the sea."

"I said he came for the sea *baths*."

"Well then! How's he going to take the sea-baths if it ain't on the sea?"

"They've got special boilers in the palace at Sheffield, and he wants his water hot. So they send the sea-water there, litres of it."

She says, "Now be honest. Ain't you telling me a lot of lies?"

"Not a lie in it," says I.

"Well then, I'll believe some of it, but I certainly won't believe it all."

Then Mary Jane steps in with Susan. "It ain't right to talk to him like that. A stranger far from his people."

"It ain't kind," says Susan, "you just ask his pardon."

"Yes," says Mary Jane, "say you're sorry."

She did it too. And she did it beautiful. I says to myself, these are the girls he's stealing money from. I felt real ashamed. And I made up my mind right then — I'll get that money back for them or burst.

So I went to the king's room and felt about in the dark. And after a time I heard their footsteps. I stood behind the curtain, and they came in and shut the door.

The duke says, "That doctor's worrying my mind. I think we'd better get out of this with what we've got. And off down the river."

"What! Without the rest of it — eight or nine thousand dollars if we sell the house and the land."

Then the duke says, "Well, we should put this money in a good place." And he pushed the money bag right in under the bedding. "It's safe for now," he says.

But before they were halfway downstairs again, I had the money out of there.

In the middle of the night, there wasn't a sound anywhere. There was only a candle-light in the room with the coffin.

I passed it by, but the front door was locked, and the key wasn't there. Just then I heard somebody coming down the stairs. I had to hide the bag, and the only place I could see was the coffin. The lid was not over the dead man's face. I pushed the money bag in under the lid, on to his chest. Then I ran across the room and hid behind the door.

Mary Jane came in and went to the coffin. She was down on her knees beside it, and looked in. Then she began to cry. I went quickly back to bed.

When I got downstairs next morning, the room with the coffin was shut. In the middle of the day, the people began to crowd in, and they talked and cried and sang a lot.

Then somebody moved the coffin lid into place and fastened it down tight. I didn't even know if the money was still in there or not.

They buried Peter and we came back home. The king was saying he had to get back to England in a hurry — his church needed him. And he said he would take the girls home with him.

The next day, a couple of men came, and the king sold them Peter Wilks's negroes. And away they went, two sons up the river, and their mother down the river to Orleans. No one had dreamed that the family would be separated, and the poor girls and the negroes almost broke their hearts with sadness.

Next morning the king and the duke woke me up. The king says, "Were you in my room, the night before last?"

"No sir."

"No lies now."

"It's the truth sir."

The duke says, "Have you seen anybody else go in there? Stop and think."

"Well, only the negroes a few times."

Both of them gave a little jump.

"Is something wrong?" I said.

The king turns on me and says, "You keep

your head shut. And mind your own business."

The two of them went off.

I didn't like to put the blame on the negroes, but it couldn't hurt them now.

11

At getting-up time I started downstairs. As I passed the girls' room, Mary Jane was sitting with her head in her hands, crying.

It was the negroes, she said. "Oh dear, dear, they ain't *ever* going to see each other any more."

Suddenly I made up my mind. "Miss Mary Jane, is there any place out of town where you could stay for a while?"

"Yes — Mr Lothrop's. Why?"

"Those negroes *will* see each other again — inside of two weeks — here in this house. If I *prove* it to you, will you go to Mr Lothrop's for a while?"

"I'll stay a year!" she says.

"All right," I says. "Now here's the truth. Those uncles of yours ain't your uncles at all. They're a couple of snakes. There. That's the worst of it."

It shocked her of course, and her eyes were on fire.

"Stay at Mr Lothrop's till nine or half-past tonight," I says. "Then come back. If I'm not here, it means I'm out of the way and safe. Then you come out and spread the news, and get these snakes into prison."

"I'll do it," she says.

"If you want people with proof, well, I'll tell you where to find them. Just send to Bricksville and mention the Royal Nonesuch — the whole town will be here before you can take a breath. And they'll be boiling too!"

Then I says, "Don't worry. These two snakes ain't your real uncles, so they *can't* sell your house. And the negroes will have to come back, because selling them wasn't lawful either."

"Well all right, but why do you want me to go to Mr Lothrop's?" she says.

"Because you ain't one of these leather-face people. Anybody can read your face like a book. Do you think you can put on some *real* smiles when your *uncles* come to kiss you good morning?"

"I'll go!"

"There's just one thing — that bag of money." I wrote on a piece of paper *I put it in the coffin.* "You can read that on the road to Mr Lothrop's," I said.

Late that afternoon a steamboat landed, and in two minutes up comes a crowd, shouting and laughing. They were fetching along a very nice-looking old gentleman, and a nice-looking young one with his right arm in a bandage.

The crowd was singing out, "Here's *another* Harvey and William Wilks. Now we've got two sets of them. You pay your money and take your choice!"

12

I thought our pair would hide away. But no. The duke just went about *goo-gooing*. And the king just looked sorrowful at the thought of two more wrongdoers in the world.

The old gentleman who'd just come began to speak. And right away he pronounced *like an Englishman*, not the king's way. "My brother has broken his arm," he says, "and we have had great troubles — our luggage got put off the boat at another town last night by mistake."

The king laughs and says, "Broken his arm — very likely, *ain't* it? Very useful. Now we don't know if he can make signs or not. Lost their luggage? That's *real* good — very clever!"

Then a big rough man comes up and says to the king, "If you're Harvey Wilks, when did you come to this town?"

"Two evenings ago, on the steamboat from Cincinnati."

"Well then, why were you up the river *that morning* — in a canoe?"

"Not me, my friend."

"It's a lie. I *saw* him there. With Tom Collins and a boy. And that's the boy there."

He pointed to me. They took us to a big room

in the hotel, and they fetched in the new couple.

A sharp-looking man came forward: it was Levi Bell the lawyer. He brought out a paper and pen, and the king wrote something, then the duke.

Then the lawyer pulled a lot of old letters out of his pocket and says, "These old letters are from the real Harvey Wilks. And here's *these* two's handwriting. Anybody can see *they* didn't write them."

Then he asked the new couple to write something. And Levi Bell says, "Anybody can tell *this* old gentleman didn't write them either."

The new old gentleman says, "Nobody can ever read my writing. So my brother here always copies for me. It's *his* writing you've got there."

"*Well,*" says the lawyer, "I've got some of William's letters too, so if you'll...."

"He's broken his arm," says the old gentleman, "and he *can't* write with his left hand. But look at both sets of letters and you'll see they're the same. William wrote them all."

"Well," says the lawyer, "this *is* a state of things."

"I've thought of something," says the old gentleman. He turns to the king and says, "Perhaps this gentleman here can tell me the marks on the left side of my brother Peter's chest? Inked into the skin."

The king whitened a little, and it was suddenly very quiet in there. But soon he began to smile, and says, "I can tell you that. It's that best-known of all Indian weapons — an arrow. A picture of a small, thin, blue arrow. If you don't look close, you can't see it."

The old gentleman says, "Who laid out the body?"

Ab Turner says, "I did. And I didn't see any such mark."

"Good!" says the old gentleman. "What you *did* see was three letters: P-B-W. Ain't that right?"

Ab Turner says, "No, we *didn't*. We never saw any marks at all."

Well, everybody *was* in a state of mind now.

"The whole lot of them's trying to fool us!" somebody shouted.

But the lawyer jumps on the table and shouts, "Gentlemen! — just one word — if you PLEASE! There's one way yet — let's go and dig up the body and look."

"That's it," they all shouted. "Let's go!"

So they took us all along to the graveyard, with the whole town behind us. And it was getting darker and darker, but they started digging right away. And the rain started, and the wind went *swish*, but nobody took any notice. At last they got out the coffin, and began to take off the lid.

And suddenly somebody shouts out, "By jingo! Here's the bag of gold on his chest!"

Everybody let out a shout and pushed forward to get a look. And I took the chance to run for the road in the dark. I pretty well flew. When I got to the river, I untied the first canoe I saw, and reached the raft waiting at a little island in the middle.

I jumped on to it and sang out, "Out with you Jim, and set her loose! We've lost them at last."

Jim ran out of the wigwam and came for me with both arms spread for happiness. And in two seconds we were sailing down the river, and it *did* seem good to be free again.

Then I noticed a sound that I knew very well. I held my breath and listened and waited. And sure enough, it was the sound of another boat, with the king and the duke in it.

So I just lay down on the boards then and gave up. And I could hardly stop myself from crying.

We daren't stop again at any town for days and days. We just kept right along down the river. We were down south in the warm weather now, and a long way from home.

The duke and the king never did agree about the money. "D'you think I'm a fool?" says the duke. "Don't you think *I* know who hid that money in the coffin?"

"I know you *do* know — because you did it yourself!"

"It's a lie!"

"Take your hands off!"

But they were soon friends again, and they started up their foolishness in the villages again. They gave a talk against drink (but they didn't make enough money to get drunk with). They started a dancing school (but the public jumped in and danced them out of town). They tried doctoring, and telling the future. And just sailing along and thinking.

One morning early, the king went on shore to look at another village, and he still wasn't back by midday. So me and the duke, we went and hunted for him.

We found him in the back room of a little bar, drunk. He couldn't walk, and the duke began to shout at him, and he shouted back. While they were busy, I saw my chance, and raced away back to the river.

"Set her loose, Jim," I sang out. "We're all right now!"

But there was no answer, and nobody came out of the wigwam. Jim was gone!

13

Pretty soon I was out on the road, and I came across a boy. I asked him if he'd seen a strange negro.

"Yes."

"Whereabouts?" says I.

"Down at Silas Phelps's place, three kilometres below here. He's a runaway negro, and they've got him."

So I set out for there, and when I got to the Phelps's farm it was all still and Sunday-like, and hot and sunshiny. Phelps's place had a big yard with some grass, but mostly smooth earth. A big house for the white people, and three little negro-cabins at the back. Outside the yard, a garden, then the cotton-fields. And after the fields, the woods.

I went for the kitchen at the back of the house, and a crowd of dogs came for me. I stopped and kept still. A negro woman comes racing out and shouting at them. And a white woman came running from the house, and little white children behind her. She was smiling all over.

"It's *you* at last! *Ain't* it?"

I said, "Yes ma'am," before I thought.

She took me in her arms and the tears came in her eyes. "You don't look much like your mother, but I'm *so* glad to see you! Children, it's your cousin — say hello."

She took me inside and sat me on a chair. She held both of my hands and said, "What kept you so long? Trouble with the boat?"

I didn't know what to say. "Yes ma'am. Part of the engine. A big bang of some sort."

"Oh dear. Anybody hurt?"

"No ma'am. Killed a negro."

"Well that's lucky, because sometimes people do get hurt. Where's your luggage, child?"

"I left it at the boat, ma'am."

"Don't say ma'am. Say Aunt Sally."

"Yes, Aunt Sally."

"And look — here's your Uncle Silas now. He's been out looking for you."

I wanted to get hold of one of the children, and find out who I was. But it was too late now.

The old gentleman came in and stared at me.

"Who's that?" he asked.

"It's *Tom Sawyer!*"

By jingo! I almost fell through the floor.

The old man shook me by the hand, and the woman danced around and laughed and cried, and they both fired off questions about the family — the Sawyer family.

Being Tom Sawyer was easy and comfortable, but then I heard a steamboat coughing along the river. And I says to myself, suppose Tom Sawyer is coming on that boat? And suppose he steps in here any minute and sings out my name? I must go up the road and stop him.

So I told them I would go and fetch my luggage. And I set off alone with the horse and wagon. Halfway to town I saw another wagon coming, and sure enough Tom Sawyer was in it.

"Hold on!" I says.

He stopped and his mouth opened like a suitcase and stayed that way. Then after a while he says, "You're dead. You just get back where you came from. I ain't ever hurt you. You know that. Why've you come back to visit me?"

I says, "I ain't come back. I ain't ever been *gone.*"

"Looky here, weren't you ever murdered *at all*?"

"No. You come here and feel me if you don't believe me."

So he did it and that was all right. I told him about the whole grand adventure. And I said,

"I'm trying to steal a negro back — old Miss Watson's Jim."

His eyes lit up and he says, "I'll *help* you!"

Well, that worried me. I know Tom Sawyer — he loves adventures. And if there ain't one there, he makes one! It's all those books he reads, giving him strange ideas.

He thought for a bit, then he says, "I know. Take my luggage in your wagon, and say it's yours. You go back, and I'll follow a half hour after."

Well, I drove back, and in about half an hour Tom's wagon came up to the house.

Aunt Sally says, "I wonder who that is? I do believe it's a stranger."

"Sid Sawyer," says Tom. "Hello, Aunt Sally!"

Well, she jumped up and ran to him and kissed him half to death. "Well! I've never seen such a surprise. We knew Tom was coming. But your Aunt Polly didn't write us about you, Sid."

"I just begged and begged, and at the last minute she let me come too."

We all had dinner, and there was enough on the table for seven families. There was a considerable lot of talk all the afternoon, and Tom and me listened hard.

But nobody said anything about a runaway negro.

14

Tom and me had to sleep in the same room and bed. So, being tired, we said goodnight and went straight up to bed after supper.

After a while Tom says to me, "Looky here, Huck, I know where Jim probably is."

"Where?"

"In that little cabin-place out at the back. When we were at dinner, didn't you see a negro man go in there with some food?"

"Yes. I supposed it was for a dog."

"Well it wasn't. Part of it was a plate of fruit. And the negro unlocked the cabin door when he went in. And he locked it again when he came out. He fetched uncle the key. A plate of fruit means a man. And a lock means a prisoner. And that prisoner's Jim. Just you think about it."

What a head for a boy to have!

"Well then," I says, "the plan is this. I get my canoe tomorrow night, and fetch the raft from the island. Then we steal the key from the old man's trousers after he goes to bed. Then we all push off down the river. Wouldn't that plan work?"

"*Work*? Certainly it would work. But what sort of adventure's that? It's far too simple. It wouldn't make any more talk than stealing a bar o' soap."

I never said anything, because I knew Tom must have a better plan. He always had.

"We'll *dig* him out," he says. "It'll take about a week!"

In the morning we were up at daybreak. We went along to be friendly with the negro that fed Jim (if it *was* Jim). He said his name was Nat. He let us go along with him and look at the prisoner.

Inside the cabin we could hardly see anything, it was so dark. But Jim was there, sure enough. Tom whispers to him quick, "You don't know us, Jim. Remember that. And if you hear any digging, it's just us. We're going to set you free."

Jim didn't say anything, but he didn't look too happy. — He knew Tom Sawyer and his plans.

Until breakfast we went to the woods to make some plans.

"First," I says, "there's this chain 'round Jim's leg. It's tied to the leg of that old bed in there."

"I know. We've got to hunt for something to make a saw."

"What do we want a saw for?" I says.

"To saw the leg off the bed."

"But you just need to lift the bed up, and the chain's free."

"Ain't you ever read any books *at all*, Huck Finn? All the best heroes have to saw the leg of their prison bed in two. Then they tie a rope to the top of the castle wall. Then you just need to climb down it and break a leg when you fall in the water at the bottom — because a rope is always ten metres too short, you know. Then your friends throw you across a horse, and away you go, back to your own country."

"There's no ring of water round Jim's cabin," I says.

"We'll dig one."

I says, "Why do we want water, when we're going to pull him out from *under* the cabin?"

But he never heard me. He was thinking again. Pretty soon he says, "No, there ain't no need for it."

"For what?" I says.

"To saw Jim's leg off."

"*What*?" I says. "Why on earth would you want to do that?"

"It happens to some of the best people. When they can't get the chain off, they cut off a hand. A leg would be even better. But I don't think we've enough need in this case. And Jim's a negro — he wouldn't understand it's the custom in Europe. But there's one thing — he *can* have a rope. We can tear up bedsheets and make one. And we can send it to him in a pie. And I've eaten worse pies."

"But Tom Sawyer, how you talk!" I says. "Jim ain't got any use for a rope. What can he *do* with it?"

"*Do* with it? He can hide it in his bed, can't he? Ain't it there for a clue, after he's gone? And don't you want to leave *any* clues? That would be a *pretty* state of things, *wouldn't* it? I never heard of such a thing."

"Well," I says, "if it's in the rules, and he's got to have it — all right, let him have it."

Then he had another idea. "We've got to borrow a shirt too."

"Why do we want a shirt, Tom?"

"For Jim to write his thoughts on."

"Jim *can't* write!"

"He can make marks on the shirt, can't he? We can make a pen for him out of an old spoon."

"Well then, what'll we make the ink out of?"

"All the best prisoners use their own blood. Jim can do that. And when he wants to send any common ordinary mysterious message for help, he can write it on the bottom of a tin plate with a fork. And he can throw it out of the window."

"Jim ain't got any tin plates."

"We can get him some."

"But nobody'll be able to *read* his plates."

"You don't *have* to be able to read it, Huck Finn. Half the time, you can't read what *anybody* writes on a tin plate."

15

After breakfast that morning, we saw some washing hanging on a clothes-line to dry. I borrowed a sheet and a white shirt.

"Now all we need is tools," says Tom.

"Tools for what?"

"To dig with. We ain't going to dig him out with our teeth, are we? We need knives."

"*Knives*! Now that's just foolish, Tom."

"I don't care. All the prisoners in the book dig with knives. And not through soil, but generally through rock. And it takes them weeks and weeks and weeks, and for ever and ever. One of those French prisoners was digging for *thirty-seven years* — and he came out in China."

"Jim doesn't know anybody in China."

"That has nothing to do with it."

"Tom," I says, "there's an old saw lying beside the back of the house. That would be a lot easier."

He looked sad and disappointed. "You never learn, Huck, do you? Just run along and hunt up some knives — three of them."

So I did it.

As soon as everybody was asleep that night, we climbed out of our room. We went to the cabin and dug and dug with our knives, till almost midnight. Our hands were really aching, and you could hardly see any result for it.

At last I says, "This ain't a thirty-seven-year job, Tom Sawyer. It's a thirty-eight-year job."

He thought a bit, then he says, "It ain't any use, Huck. We've just got to get some proper digging-tools. But we can think of them *as if* they're just knives."

So we fetched some old farm tools and started digging. In about three hours, the job was done. We went in and came up under Jim's bed.

Jim was asleep and we had to wake him up. He almost cried for happiness, and said we could break the chain and get out of there at once. But Tom showed him how that was not regular, and broke all the rules for escaping. Tom said there was plenty of time, and he told Jim our plans.

Jim told us Uncle Silas and Aunt Sally came in every day or two to see him. So Tom says to Jim, "We'll put small things in their pockets, and you must steal them out."

Jim had plenty of pipes, so we had a smoke and a real good friendly time. Then Tom and me, we came out through the hole again and went back to bed.

Next day Tom stole a spoon for Jim to make a pen with. And I stole three tin plates from the slaves' cabins. And in the kitchen, we found the negro cook Nat, and I took him to one side and talked to him. Meanwhile Tom pushed the spoon into the middle of a piece of corn bread.

We went along to see how it would work. It worked just fine and Jim soon found it. In fact when he bit into the corn bread, he almost broke his teeth out.

Tom and me, we then went to the rubbish pile in the back yard, and found an old tin wash-pan. It was big enough to bake a considerable size pie in. Then Tom found a couple of iron nails: he said a prisoner could use them to write his name and sorrows on the walls.

He dropped one nail into Aunt Sally's pocket,

and he pushed the other into the band of Uncle Silas's hat. Then we dropped the spoon into Uncle Silas's coat pocket.

We went in the house, and Aunt Sally was saying, "Silas, I've hunted high and I've hunted low, and I just *don't* know where your other shirt is. It was on the clothes-line yesterday. *And* there's a spoon gone."

Just then the negro woman steps in and says, "Missus, one of the sheets has gone."

"A *sheet*!"

"She was on the clothes-line yesterday, and she's not there now."

Aunt Sally was just a-boiling. Then Uncle Silas, looking foolish, fished that spoon out of his pocket. Tom and me, we decided to go quietly away till the storm was over. Just as we were going, the old man took up his hat and the nail fell on the floor. He just picked it up and laid it on the table and said nothing, and went out.

Then Tom wanted to steal another spoon. We dropped it in Aunt Sally's pocket while she was still on the boil. And Jim got it, along with her nail, before noon.

At night Jim helped us to tear up the sheet and tie it all together. And long before daylight we had a lovely rope.

But that pie was a job. We fixed it up in the woods and baked it there. But there was rope enough for forty pies, and plenty left over for soup and sausage. But Uncle Silas had a big warming-pan, and we used that. Nat agreed to take the pie in for Jim's food. And we put the tin plates in the bottom of the pan.

So Jim got everything all right. When he was by himself, he broke into the pie, hid the rope under the bed, made some marks on a tin plate and threw it out of the window.

Just before midnight me and Tom were talking. He said, "You know, the walls in that cabin just ain't right."

"How d'you mean, Tom."

"They don't have wooden walls in a real prison. Prisoners always write their words into rock."

"There ain't any there, Tom."

"We'll fetch a rock."

We went hunting about and around, and we found a great flat stone. We tried to roll it back to the cabin, but it was a real hard job. It kept falling over. We got halfway, but it was no use.

So we went to fetch Jim. He raised up his bed and pulled the chain off the bed leg. He hung the chain round his neck, and we all left through the hole. Jim and me moved that stone along, and Tom was in charge. Tom knew everything about being in charge.

The stone was a bit too big for the hole, but Jim soon made the hole big enough, and pushed the stone under his bed.

We helped him to fix his chain back on the bed leg, and then we were ready for bed ourselves.

16

Well, by the end of three weeks, everything was in pretty good shape.

The shirt was sent in early in another pie. The bed leg was sawed in two, and we ate up all the wood dust, and it gave us a powerful ache inside. It was the worst wood dust I ever tasted.

Tom said, "Now's the time for the mysterious message."

"What message?" I said.

"Warnings to people that something's going to happen."

"But looky here, Tom, what do we want to *warn* them for? Let them find out for themselves."

"You just can't depend on them. They don't take any notice of anything at all. So if we don't *give* them notice, nobody'll try to stop us. And this escape'll go off perfectly flat and easy. And we don't want *that*."

So Tom wrote a letter and pushed it under the front door at the first light of day. This letter said:

I wish to be your friend. There is a dangerous lot of criminals over in Indian country. They are going to steal your runaway negro tonight. I am one of them, but I wish to leave them and lead an honest life again. So I am telling you this terrible plan of theirs. They will come from the north at midnight with a false key. And they will go to the negro's cabin and get him. While they are getting his chains loose, you can lock them in, and then you can kill them any way you want. I do not want any payment for this, but I know I have done the right thing.

UNKNOWN FRIEND

I never saw a family in such a fright. If a door banged, Aunt Sally jumped and said, "Ouch!" If anything fell, she jumped and said, "Ouch!" If you touched her when she wasn't noticing, she did the same. She was afraid to go to bed, but she daren't sit up.

After supper I opened the door of the sitting-room and walked in. What a crowd! Fifteen farmers, and every one of them had a gun. Aunt Sally sent me straight up to bed, but I was upstairs in a second and out of the window in another.

I ran straight to Jim's cabin. Tom was waiting there, and I told him, "We've got to jump as quick as we can. *Now.* And not a minute to lose — the house is full of men with guns!"

His eyes just lit up and he says, "*Ain't* it wonderful! If I did it all again, I could probably fetch two hundred! Maybe if we could put it off till...."

"*Hurry*," I says. "Where's Jim?"

"Right at your side there."

Then we heard the footsteps of men coming

to the door. And we heard the men handling the lock.

A man said, "I *told* you we'd be too soon. They haven't come yet — this door is locked. Here, I'll lock some of you inside the cabin. You wait for them in the dark, and kill them when they come."

So in they came, but they couldn't see us in the dark, and they almost stood on us while we were rushing under the bed. But we got under all right, and out through the hole at the back of the cabin, quick but quiet.

We went across to the wooden railing, but Tom's trousers caught on the top rail. He had to pull loose, which made a noise.

And somebody sings out, "Who's that? Answer or I'll shoot!"

But we didn't answer. We just ran.

Then there was a rush, and a *bang bang bang*! and the bullets flew around us.

We heard somebody sing out, "There they are! They're going for the river! After them, boys! And set the dogs loose!"

The dogs came racing, and made enough noise for a million. But they were our dogs, so we just stopped till they came up. And when they saw it was us, they only just said *hello-there* and raced ahead.

We went off through the bushes to my canoe. We jumped in and set off for the middle of the river. And we soon arrived at the island where my raft was.

We were all as glad as could be. But Tom was

the gladdest of all, because he had a bullet in his leg.

17

Well, that was the end of Tom's silly adventure. There was nothing else to do — I just had to go back for a doctor, while Jim stayed and looked after Tom. And by morning, we were all back at Uncle Silas's again.

Tom was brought back on a board, and Jim's hands were tied behind his back.

Aunt Sally threw herself at Tom, crying, and says, "Oh, he's dead, he's dead, I know he's dead!"

And Tom turned his head a little and whispered something. And she threw up her arms and says, "He's alive!" And she planted a kiss on him.

Some of the men wanted to hang Jim. But the others said, "Don't do that, he ain't *our* negro. And his owner'll just come along and make us pay for him."

So they took Jim to the same cabin and chained him again, but this time both hands and both legs to a huge piece of wood.

When Aunt Sally told Tom that, he rose up in bed, with his eye hot, and sings out to me, "They ain't got any *right* to shut him up! *Push off*, Huck, and don't you lose a minute. Set him loose! He doesn't belong to anybody — he's as free as anyone on this earth!"

"What *does* the child mean?" says Aunt Sally.

"I mean every word I *say*, Aunt Sally. And if somebody doesn't go, *I'll* go. I've known Jim all his life, and so has Tom there. Old Miss Watson died two months ago. And she was real ashamed of wanting to sell him. And she *said* so. And she wrote out a paper that set him free."

"Then why on earth did *you* want to set him free, if he was free already?"

"Well, that *is* a question, I must say. And *just* like a woman! I wanted the *adventure* of it of course. And I — AUNT POLLY!"

And sure enough, Tom's Aunt Polly was right there, just inside the door. Aunt Sally jumped for her, and almost kissed the head off her. And I found a good enough place for me under the bed.

Aunt Polly looked across at Tom and says, "Yes, you'd *better* turn your head away, Tom!"

"Oh dear," says Aunt Sally, "but that ain't *Tom*. It's Sid. Tom is — where is Tom?"

"You mean, where's Huck Finn — *that's* what you mean! Don't worry. I know these two when I see them. Come out from under that bed, Huck Finn."

So I did it. Aunt Sally didn't know up from down. So Tom's Aunt Polly, she told all about who I was, and then I had to explain my part of it.

Aunt Polly said, "Well now, Sally. You wrote to me and said Tom *and Sid* had come all right

and safe. So I says to myself, Well now! Now I just have to go sailing all the way down the river, fifteen hundred kilometres, and find out what's going on *this* time."

We had Jim out of the chains in no time, and Aunt Sally gave him a good time, and all he wanted to eat. And Jim and me, we went up to see Tom in his room.

And Tom says, "Let's all three of us push along out of here, one of these nights, and go for adventures among the Indians for a couple of weeks."

And I said, "I ain't got any money left for that kind of journey. And I won't get any from home. My dad must have got it all away from Judge Thatcher. And by now he must have drunk it all up."

"No, he hasn't," Tom says. "It's all still there — six thousand dollars and more. And your dad's never been back since."

Jim looked a bit serious, and he says, "He ain't coming back any more, Huck."

"Why, Jim?"

"Never mind why, Huck. But he ain't coming back."

But I kept asking him, so at last he says, "Don't you remember that house that was sailing down the river? And there was a man in there, covered up? And I went and uncovered him, and I wouldn't let you in? Well then, you can get your money when you want it, because that was your dad."

18

Tom's almost well now, and he keeps the bullet round his neck. And everything's all right again, so there's nothing more to write about. And I'm sure glad about *that* — if I knew all the trouble of writing a book, I wouldn't have started it. And I ain't going to do any more.

But I'm thinking I'll set out for Indian country ahead of the rest of them. Aunt Sally says she's going to be a mother to me, and teach me good manners and proper behaviour.

And that's too much for me — I've been there before.

THE END
YOURS TRULY
HUCK FINN

A Puzzle

Would you like to try a puzzle? We've written 36 sentences for you. Every sentence has one word in BIG LETTERS: the letters of that word have been changed around. For example:—

We built a GIMWAW to keep us dry. The word GIMWAW should be *wigwam*. Find the right word for each sentence. Then put the *first letter* of that word at its proper number in the answer at the end of the puzzle. We've done the first one for you already. The answer is something else that Mark Twain wrote.

1   We built a GIMWAW to keep us dry.
2   A wooden EUSHO came slowly down the river.
3   The villagers brought bad SEGG and cabbages.
4   Tom hid a LIAN in Aunt Sally's pocket.
5   "That man TINA asleep – he's dead."
6   Jim was Miss Watson's GRONE.
7   The king liked a private SLAGS of whisky.
8   Huck and Jim sailed on a FRAT.
9   The moneybag was full of WOLLEY coins.
10 Huck and his dad stayed in a wood INBAC.
11 The duke found a printing COIFFE.
12 Tom wanted to pull Jim from DRUNE the cabin.
13 Huck and Jim travelled at THINGS.
14 Huck shot a pig and cut its HATTOR.
15 Huck's father was about TIFFY.
16 The duke said Huck TOUGH to bend low to him.
17 Aunt Sally's husband was CLUNE Silas.
18 An exciting play – the LAYOR Nonesuch!
19 Tom Sawyer was driving a horse and GANOW.
20 Huck took a SHORE shoe from the house in the river.
21 At night Huck went ashore for things to TEA.
22 Most green grows on the THORN side of a tree.
23 The Nonesuch was in a GALEVIL hall.
24 The king said he must return to DANGLEN.

25 Huck used a canoe to cross the VERRI.

26 "Peter Wilks died ATDRYEYES evening."

27 The best-known of Indian weapons: an OWRAR.

28 "I'd VEERN seen so much money in one place."

29 "Trouble has brought these ERGY hairs."

30 "We can tie Jim up with a PORE."

31 "OUREY going to feel sick when you think of this day."

32 Jim didn't want to be a VALSE any more.

33 Huck learned to TIREW at school.

34 "Selling the negroes wasn't lawful HEERIT."

35 FRATE supper, Joanna talked with Huck.

36 Huck tried to hit the STAR with some metal.

$$\overline{1}\ \overline{2}\ \overline{3}\ \overline{4}\quad \overline{5}\ \overline{6}\ \overline{7}\ \overline{8}\ \overline{9}\ '\quad \overline{10}\ \overline{11}\ \overline{12}\ \overline{13}\ \overline{14}$$

$$\overline{15}\ \overline{16}\ \overline{17}\ \overline{18}\ :\quad \overline{19}\ \overline{20}\ \overline{21}\ \overline{22}\quad \overline{23}\ \overline{24}\ \overline{25}\ \overline{26}$$

$$\overline{27}\ \overline{28}\ \overline{29}\ \overline{30}\ \overline{31}\ '\quad \overline{32}\ \overline{33}\ \overline{34}\ \overline{35}\ \overline{36}\ .$$

Answers

1 wigwam 2 house 3 eggs 4 nail 5 ain't
6 negro 7 glass 8 raft 9 yellow 10 cabin
11 office 12 under 13 nights 14 throat
15 fifty 16 ought 17 uncle 18 royal
19 wagon 20 horse 21 eat 22 north
23 village 24 England 25 river 26 yesterday
27 arrow 28 never 29 grey 30 rope
31 you're 32 slave 33 write 34 either
35 after 36 rats

80